Lida Kindersley

Fun With
a b c

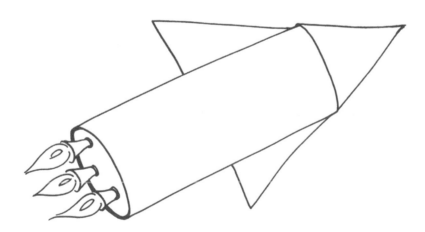

OXFORD
UNIVERSITY PRESS

Introduction

These workbooks introduce and reinforce basic numeracy and literacy concepts for pre-school and Reception Year children. They give children opportunities to develop some of the skills that act as a springboard for the Foundation Stage Profile, an assessment which teachers complete on each child before he or she moves into Year 1. The activities should be fun and are designed to stimulate discussion as well as practical skills. Some children will be able to complete activities alone, after initial discussion; others may benefit from adult support throughout.

Fun with abc offers activities which help children to:

- learn the order of letters in the alphabet
- recognize individual lower case letters
- learn the names of the letters and the sounds they make
- practise individual letter formation

Oxford University Press
Great Clarendon Street, Oxford OX2 6DP

Oxford University Press is a department of the University of Oxford.
It furthers the University's objective of excellence in research, scholarship, and education by publishing worldwide in
Oxford New York Auckland Cape Town Dar es Salaam Hong Kong Karachi
Kuala Lumpur Madrid Melbourne Mexico City Nairobi New Delhi Shanghai
Taipei Toronto

With offices in
Argentina Austria Brazil Chile Czech Republic France Greece Guatemala
Hungary Italy Japan Poland Portugal Singapore South Korea Switzerland
Thailand Turkey Ukraine Vietnam

Oxford is a registered trade mark of ©Oxford University Press
in the UK and in certain other countries

© Lida Kindersley 2006
The moral rights of the author have been asserted
Database right Oxford University Press (maker)
First published 2006

British Library Cataloguing in Publication Data
Data available

ISBN-10: 0-19-838567-6
ISBN-13: 978-0-19-838567-7

Pack of 6
ISBN-10: 0-19-838568-4
ISBN-13: 978-0-19-838568-4

Pack of 36
ISBN-10: 0-19-838569-2
ISBN-13: 978-0-19-838569-1

1 3 5 7 9 10 8 6 4 2

Designed by Red Face Design
Illustrations by Lida Kindersley
Printed in China

PACKS ARE NOT YET PUBLISHED.

Contents

Note to parents 4

The alphabet 5

The letter a 6

The letter b 7

The letter c 8

The letter d 9

The letter e 10

The letter f 11

The letter g 12

The letter h 13

The letter i 14

The letter j 15

The letter k 16

The letter l 17

The letter m 18

The letter n 19

The letter o 20

The letter p 21

The letter q 22

The letter r 23

The letter s 24

The letter t 25

The letter u 26

The letter v 27

The letter w 28

The letter x 29

The letter y 30

The letter z 31

Summary of skills 32

Note to parents

From an early age, children are often fascinated by writing. They may imitate the process of writing even before they have acquired actual writing skills, by simply making marks and scribbled versions of letter shapes. It is important to encourage such activities and to increase the children's awareness of the links between writing, reading, speaking and listening.

Whenever possible, draw the children's attention to letters and words in the world around them, not just in books, but also on posters, food packaging, signs, labels, on television, on the side of vehicles, etc. By increasing their awareness of print you will help children to understand that words and letters convey meaning. You can reinforce the link between speaking, reading and writing by showing your child how you can write down their words and stories, and then read them back to them.

To develop reading and writing skills, children need to recognize letters of the alphabet, know the letter names, and also the sounds that the letters make. *Fun With a b c* provides activities to introduce and practise these basic skills. The alphabet snake on page 5 can be used in many different ways: to chant or sing the alphabet; to play games, for example by covering up a letter and asking the child which letter is missing, etc.

Pages 6 to 31 focus on different letters of the alphabet in sequence. Each page is designed to be used in the following way:

- Say the sound of the letter and the name of the picture, so 'a' for apple, 'b' for box, etc.
- Trace the shape of the letter with the child's finger, following the direction of the arrow.
- Fill the top picture with letters copied from the coloured letters; they can vary in size at this stage because the focus should be on the movement of the hand.
- Fill the bottom picture with letters, this time trying to regularize the size to the model of the black letter.
- Finally, ask the child to choose their best version of the letter, and to copy it into the coloured frame at the bottom.

Starting to Write

Before your child starts to write make sure they are sitting comfortably with a level surface in front of them. Encourage them to find a relaxed posture, by shrugging their shoulders, stretching and bending their arms and wriggling their fingers. Then give them a pencil and check that they are holding it correctly, as shown.

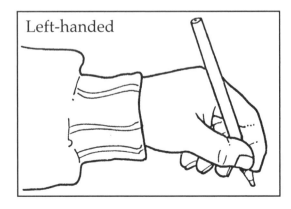

Left-handed

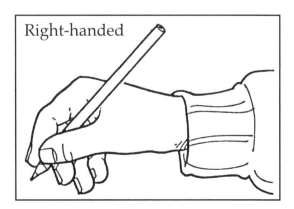

Right-handed

The alphabet

Sing or say the alphabet.

The letter a

my best a

The letter b

my best b

The letter c

my best c

The letter d

my best d

The letter e

my best e

The letter f

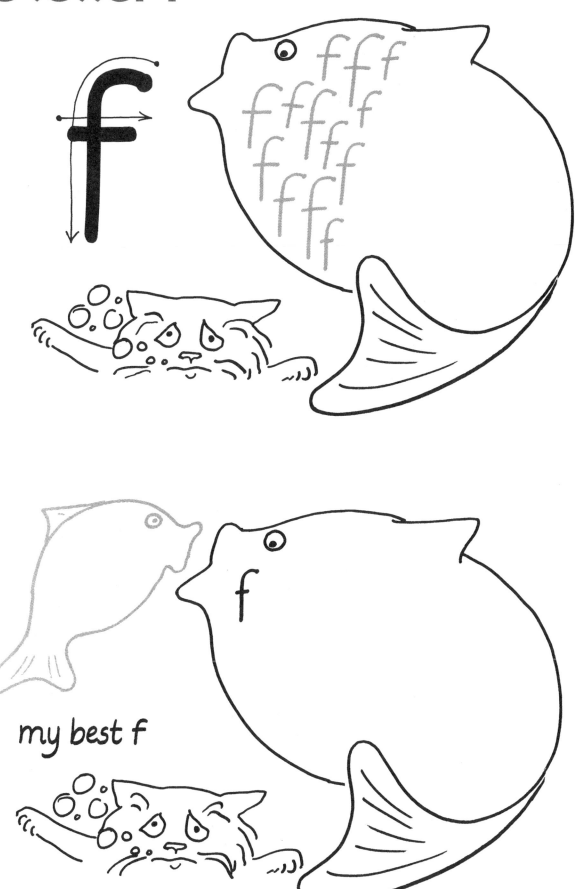

f f f
f f f f
f f f f
f f f
f f f f
f f f

my best f

11

The letter g

my best g

The letter h

my best h

The letter i

my best i

i

The letter j

my best j

j

The letter k

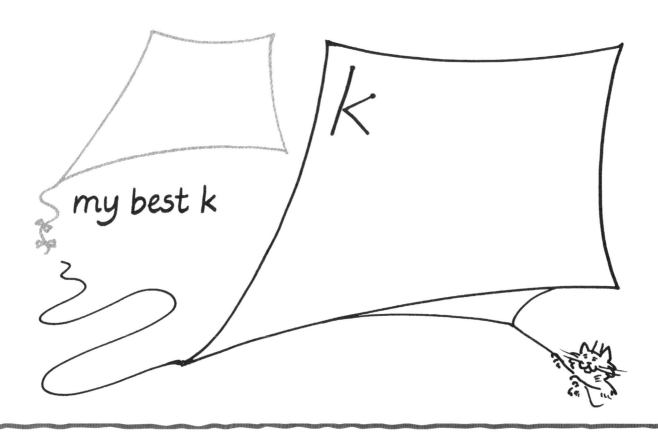

my best k

The letter l

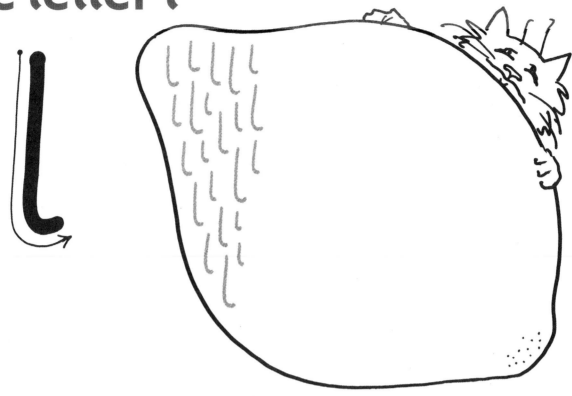

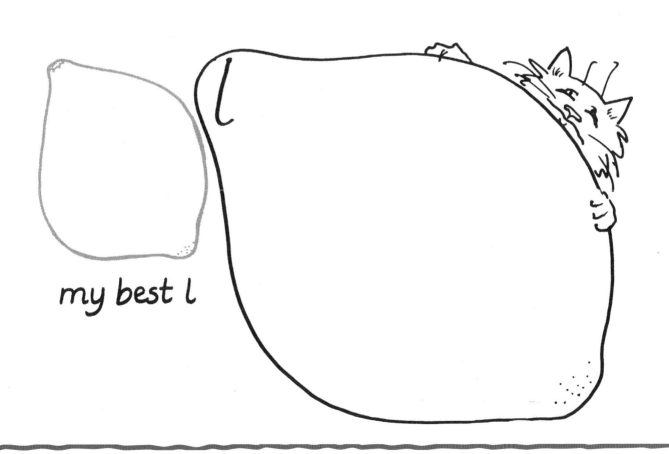

my best l

The letter m

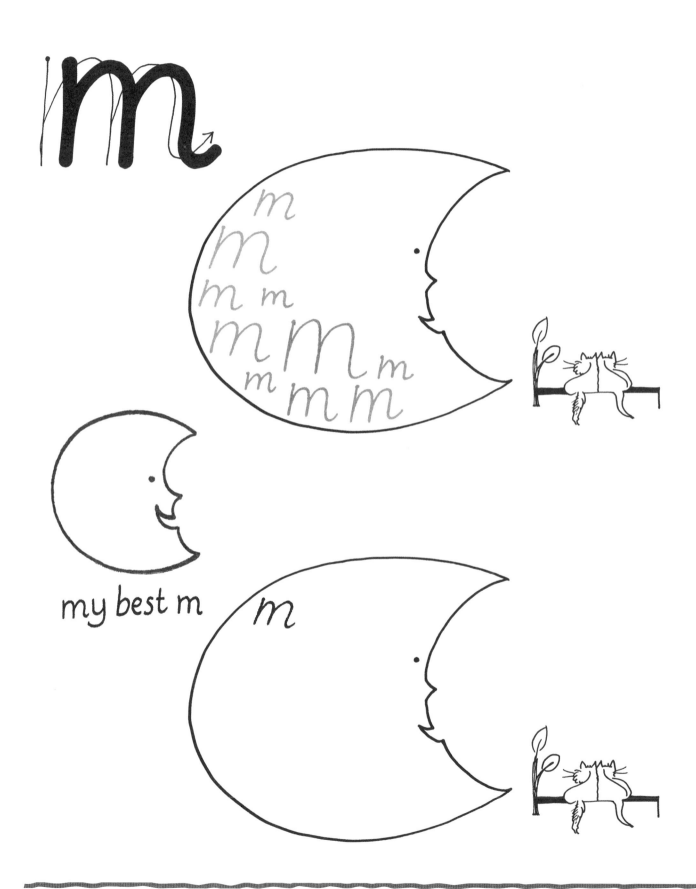

my best m

The letter n

my best n

The letter o

my best o

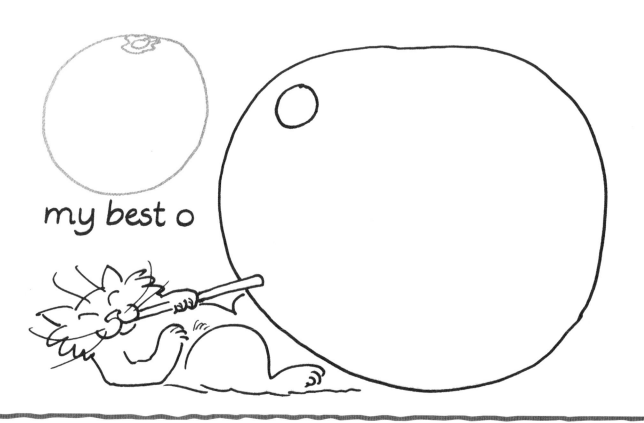

The letter p

my best p

The letter q

my best q

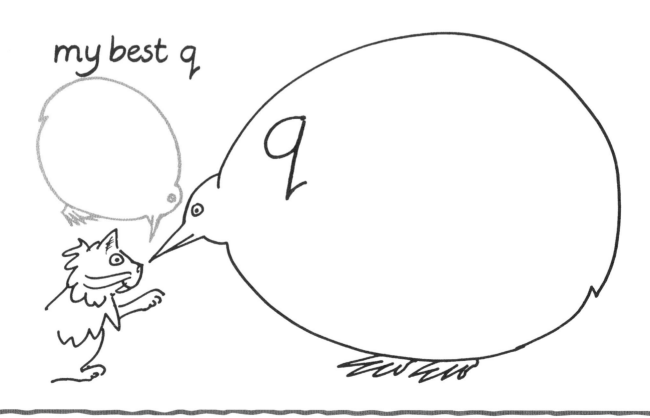

The letter r

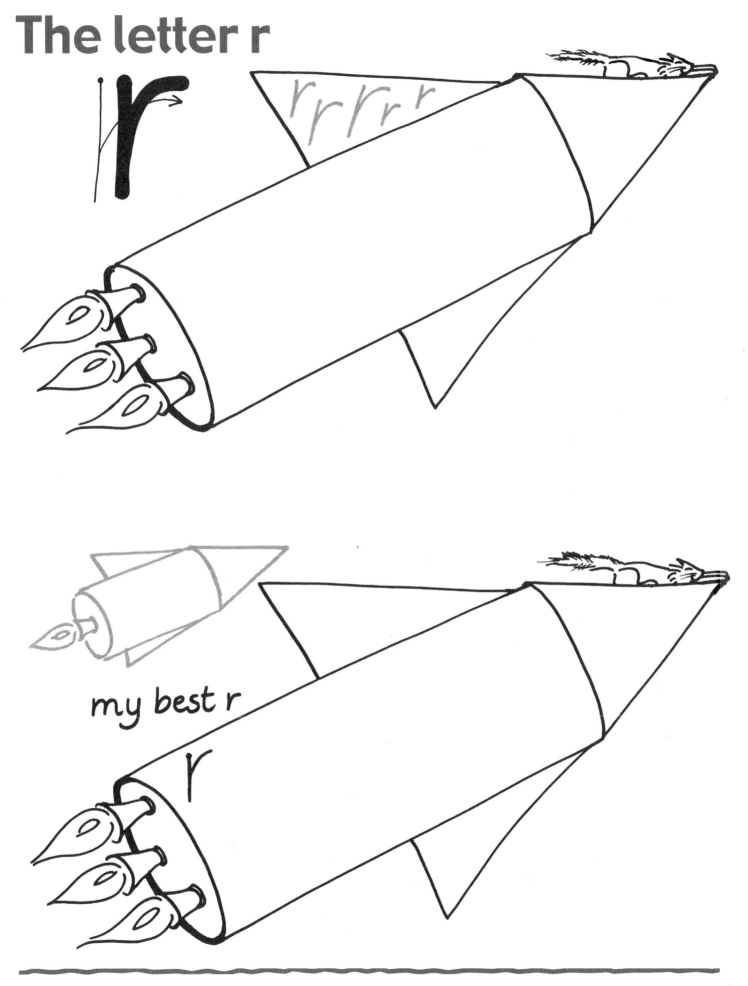

r r r r

my best r

r

The letter s

S S S S S

s

my best s

The letter t

t t t
t t
t

t

my best t

The letter u

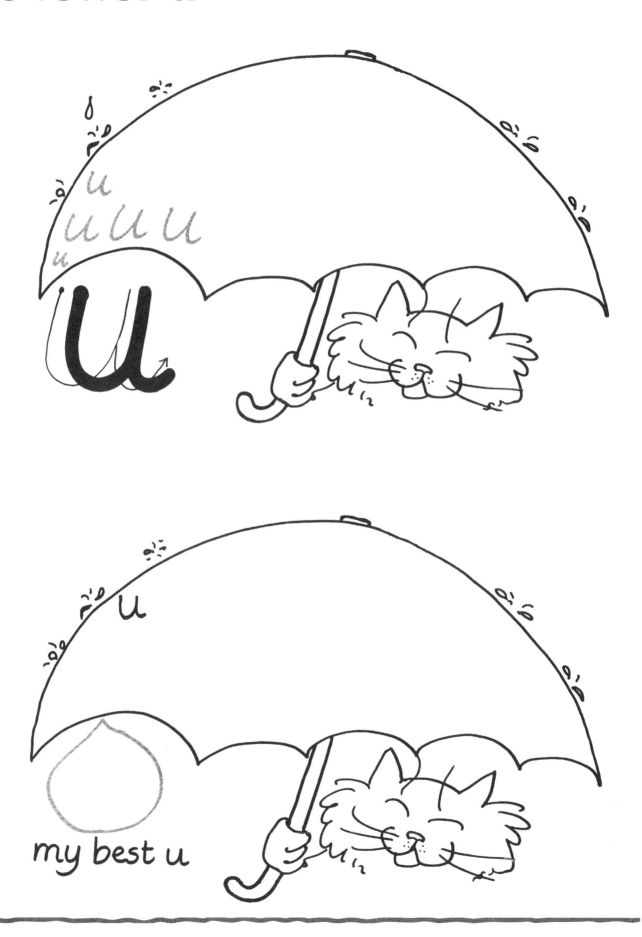

my best u

The letter v

my best v

The letter w

my best w

W

The letter x

my best x

The letter y

my best y

The letter z

my best z

Summary of skills

Title	Page	Summary
The alphabet	5	Learning the letters of the alphabet in sequence
The letter a	6	Recognizing the letter, saying the sound, writing the shape
The letter b	7	Recognizing the letter, saying the sound, writing the shape
The letter c	8	Recognizing the letter, saying the sound, writing the shape
The letter d	9	Recognizing the letter, saying the sound, writing the shape
The letter e	10	Recognizing the letter, saying the sound, writing the shape
The letter f	11	Recognizing the letter, saying the sound, writing the shape
The letter g	12	Recognizing the letter, saying the sound, writing the shape
The letter h	13	Recognizing the letter, saying the sound, writing the shape
The letter i	14	Recognizing the letter, saying the sound, writing the shape
The letter j	15	Recognizing the letter, saying the sound, writing the shape
The letter k	16	Recognizing the letter, saying the sound, writing the shape
The letter l	17	Recognizing the letter, saying the sound, writing the shape
The letter m	18	Recognizing the letter, saying the sound, writing the shape
The letter n	19	Recognizing the letter, saying the sound, writing the shape
The letter o	20	Recognizing the letter, saying the sound, writing the shape
The letter p	21	Recognizing the letter, saying the sound, writing the shape
The letter q	22	Recognizing the letter, saying the sound, writing the shape
The letter r	23	Recognizing the letter, saying the sound, writing the shape
The letter s	24	Recognizing the letter, saying the sound, writing the shape
The letter t	25	Recognizing the letter, saying the sound, writing the shape
The letter u	26	Recognizing the letter, saying the sound, writing the shape
The letter v	27	Recognizing the letter, saying the sound, writing the shape
The letter w	28	Recognizing the letter, saying the sound, writing the shape
The letter x	29	Recognizing the letter, saying the sound, writing the shape
The letter y	30	Recognizing the letter, saying the sound, writing the shape
The letter z	31	Recognizing the letter, saying the sound, writing the shape

Fun With Letter Forms

Pack of 6
ISBN-10: 0-19-838581-1

ISBN-13: 978-0-19-838581-3

Pack of 36
ISBN-10: 0-19-838582-X
ISBN-13: 978-0-19-838582-0

Fun With Pattern and Shape

Pack of 6
ISBN-10: 0-19-838575-7

ISBN-13: 978-0-19-838575-2

Pack of 36
ISBN-10: 0-19-838576-5
ISBN-13: 978-0-19-838576-9

Fun With Sounds and Rhymes

Pack of 6
ISBN-10: 0-19-838578-1

ISBN-13: 978-0-19-838578-3

Pack of 36
ISBN-10: 0-19-838579-X
ISBN-13: 978-0-19-838579-0

Fun With Colours

Pack of 6
ISBN-10: 0-19-838571-4

ISBN-13: 978-0-19-838571-4

Pack of 36
ISBN-10: 0-19-838572-2
ISBN-13: 978-0-19-838572-1

Fun With abc

**Pack of 6
ISBN-10: 0-19-838568-4**

ISBN-13: 978-0-19-838568-4

Pack of 36
ISBN-10: 0-19-838569-2
ISBN-13: 978-0-19-838569-1

PACKS ARE NOT YET PUBLISHED.